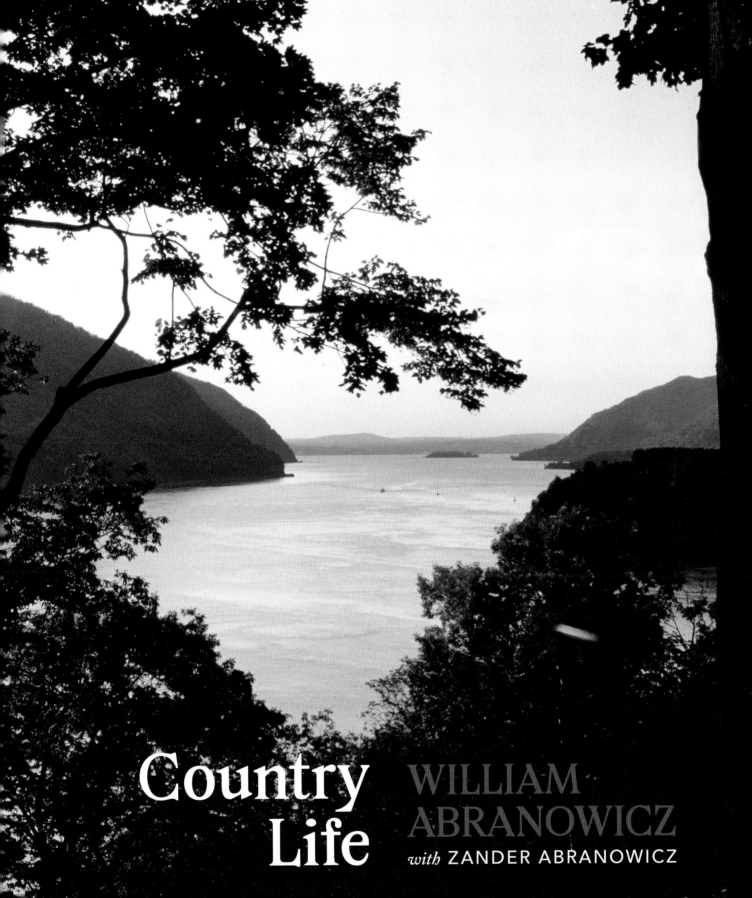

Country Life

WILLIAM ABRANOWICZ

with ZANDER ABRANOWICZ

HOMES *of the* CATSKILL MOUNTAINS
and HUDSON VALLEY

VENDOME

NEW YORK · LONDON

CONTENTS

INTRODUCTION 12

18 ALAN WANZENBERG +
PETER KELLY

MELORA KUHN 32

46 GARY TINTEROW +
CHRISTOPHER GARDNER

RON SHARKEY 60

74 MARK McDONALD +
DWAYNE RESNICK

PETER FRANK 88
+ JONATHAN LERNER

ISABEL ✝ FREDERIC CHURCH 112

GEOFF HOWELL 134

JESSICA PIAZZA ✝ TIM UNICH 160

JENNIFER McLAWHORN 184
✝ CHRISTOPHER KISSOCK

ANDREA MENKE 208
✝ CLARK SANDERS

JASON FRANK ✝ VINNIE LOPEZ 234

HAL PHILIPPS 258
✝ GREG KENDALL

98 MARIA ✝ THOMAS COLE

124 DOUG ✝ MIKE STARN

146 KATHRYN ✝ SIMONE SCOTT

172 MITA ✝ GERALD BLAND

194 ROGER ROSS WILLIAMS ✝
CASPER DE BOER

222 JOHN MARKUS

248 HANNAH LEIGHTON ✝
CHRISTIAN HARDER

270 ACKNOWLEDGMENTS

INTRODUCTION

I first visited upstate New York when I was a child living in Bayonne, New Jersey. My Aunt Rita and Uncle Harley lived on a farm near Lake George. They raised hogs and grew vegetables. My memories are vague, but one image, captured in a black-and-white photograph, remains etched in my mind. My young father is leaning against a large hog lolling on the ground as I peer curiously. Behind him is my mother, holding my baby sister Susan, who pulls back in a blur. The smile on my twenty-nine-year-old father's face reveals utter contentment in those rural surroundings, something he couldn't find readily in urban New Jersey, studying at night to become an operating engineer while working two jobs to support a family of six living in a tiny apartment. Among other things I inherited from my father is the gene that also makes me happiest in the country.

My wife, Andrea, and I live in a house high on a mountainside outside Margaretville, a village on the border of Catskill Park, a 700,000-acre swath of land deeded by New York State in 1904 to remain "forever wild." While some development is permitted, anything that infringes on the watershed of New York City is not. As we watch the light of day begin to imprint upon the ridge across the valley, the rising sun reflects in brilliant gold against the windows of the one other house we can see from our deck. I begin most days in the dark and watch the color of the sunrise evolve on those hillsides and fields. Many mornings a thick white cloud of mist slowly undulates as it rises from the bottom of the valley, where the East Branch Delaware River runs, ascending and evaporating into the light of day.

We found our way here in 2001 through friends who invited us to their 1970s A-frame ski rental in Fleischmanns, a popular vacation destination from the late 1800s through the 1950s that has now been revitalized. By the next weekend, we had found our own seasonal rental, a quintessential ski shack with an ornery porcupine who resided just a few inches below our poorly insulated floor. The house was always filled with friends. Exhausted from skiing and comfortable in our long johns, we spent the long, dark hours of winter in front of the fire with games, pizza, and movies. Our time in that shabby shack was heavenly. Many winters we averaged more than fifty days on the mountain with our three kids. We learned that leaning into winter and its pleasures made those otherwise dreaded months much more tolerable. We learned to live by the Norwegian creed *Det finnes ikke dårlig vær, bare dårlig klær!* ("There is no bad weather, only bad clothes!")

After a number of seasons renting, we decided to buy. We found thirty-six rocky hillside acres and built a small house employing the most environmentally friendly systems and materials available at the time. HGTV and *Martha Stewart Living* did video segments on the house's "green" qualities after it was completed in 2005.

During the pandemic, our isolated home became the lockdown retreat for our now-adult family, our three kids and assorted mates gathering for safety here, away from the world. When the pandemic subsided and they returned to their lives elsewhere, we decided to stay and sell our house in Bedford, New York. As empty nesters, we'd talked about parting with it for years, always looking for a sign that would tell us the time was right. COVID, and the ensuing mass exodus from New York, was that sign. It was a remarkable privilege.

We work like everyone else, with too many hours on too many devices, but we have the good fortune of going off the grid in the woods or at the pond we dug down the hill. Carrying only books, snacks, and drinks, we can tune out the minutiae of our workaday lives and tune into the sound of spring water pouring into the pond at both ends, the calls of the birds, and the ever-mesmerizing dance of light and breeze over the surface of the water. In winter the pond provides me with photographic subject matter: wind-shaped impressions of ice and snow on its surface, richly textured stone walls, and a field of reeds and goldenrod stalks that lift through the snow, emulating a giant abstract Harry Callahan photograph. We watch hawks, bald eagles, and other birds of prey circle slowly as thermal winds carry them up the New Kingston Valley toward nearby Mount Pisgah. The sounds of man—trucks and the noon siren from town—intrude rarely, allowing the delicate chatter of chipmunks, squirrels, chickadees, sparrows, blue jays, cardinals, titmice, orioles, grosbeaks, and warblers to emerge. In summer, monarchs and other pollinators flit among milkweed stalks, nourishing themselves while pollinating and laying eggs. Most mornings in season, pileated woodpeckers, those ingenious foresters, pound into dead or dying trees with a jackhammer sound that's hard to imagine coming from a head smaller than a child's fist.

With access to wide vistas, we can't help but follow the changing seasons. The shifting locus of the sun's rising and setting dramatically affects how light paints the space we live in. The movements and phases of the moon, the positions of the stars, the birds that migrate through, and the color of deer coats are all in constant flux. I find the breakdown of organic matter particularly fascinating: trillions of creatures and organisms doing their best to survive, all while enriching the earth and providing a healthy environment for us.

The elements dictate the conditions of living here. If it's too hot, we have cold streams, ponds, and rivers in which to swim. To warm ourselves, we build fires with firewood I spend a good part of the year managing. The fire in the soapstone stove we use to heat our home requires both purchased cords of firewood and fallen trees on the property, which I cut and split to add to the neat piles we watch diminish over the cold months. Firewood takes careful planning, which, as an activity, I enjoy very much. This meditative, calming, repetitive, productive mode of movement appeals to my inner compulsion to build something in a visually pleasing, perfectly pragmatic manner. The reward is fire, the heart of our winter lives.

The homes and studios I have photographed for this book are near my own. The farthest is a pleasant two-hour drive through small towns situated at the base of rolling hills, along scenic rivers, over the dramatic Kaaterskill Clove, and down across the Hudson River. On these trips I witnessed the dramatic views, weather, and light that drew Thomas Cole and Frederic Church into the mountains and continues to draw creative people en masse. The homes I chose to photograph came to me fluidly. Many belong to old friends. A few others came through introductions. I could have gone on for years and not exhausted the subjects and locations that continue to reveal themselves.

The breathtaking landscape of the Hudson Valley region was shaped by its original inhabitants, the Munsee and Mohican tribes, over more than 10,000 years. Controlled burns cleared woodlands to create fields to plant crops. Those fields and open meadows would later inspire the Hudson River School painters, who were lured by the wilderness while maintaining deep associations with the budding American conservation movement. Several of the homes in this book are located within the views in their paintings. Stewardship of land or the strong old bones of historic homes are common themes among the inhabitants included in this book. Conservation is another. In addition to the Hudson Valley's place in the formation of America as a nation, Storm King Mountain in the southern part of the valley is often seen as the birthplace of the American environmental movement.

History is a catalyst in many projects I photograph. I began making the images for this book at Thomas Cole's home. Originally thinking of photographing only in the Catskill Mountains on the western bank of the Hudson River, once I began thinking about Olana, Frederic Church's home, I found a thread to follow. Church, a student of Cole's, built his home directly across the Hudson from his mentor's. They are now connected by the Rip Van Winkle Bridge. The locations, panoramas, influences, colors, textures, and layers of both homes are echoed in many others on these pages.

Everyone in this book moved upstate to find something or to return to something that was missing for them—something on a long list of qualities that only a life in the country could satisfy. For some it was smaller communities. For others, solitude. For many, especially the artists, it was space, light, and affordability. Throughout the history of art, artists like Cole and Church have searched for a place to create that has fewer barriers, that enriches the spirit, and that endlessly inspires. They found that place here. Nature is a great muse. For those of us living here, it is about the ease of connecting to nature and its beneficent effects on all the very basic elements of us, as humans, and on the nourishment of spirit and soul. My hope is that this work becomes a small record for the future—a social document of a period, place, and people. While design and architecture are of interest to me, it is the distillation of the intangible qualities of these immensely talented people, and the ways they're inscribed into their homes, studios, and properties, that lit a fire in me. I hope it does the same for you.

ALAN WANZENBERG ✝ PETER KELLY

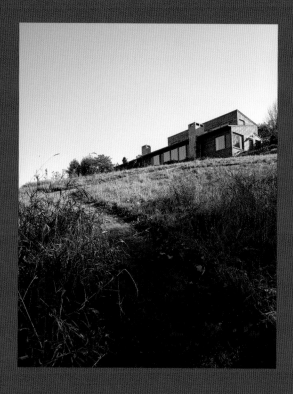

The map told me I'd arrived, but I still had a ways to go. I'd driven the half-mile gravel road through a forest of birch, ash, and oak to the home of architect and designer Alan Wanzenberg and landscape architect Peter Kelly many times before. Each time, the long approach surprises me. I first visited in 2009 for German *Architectural Digest* to photograph the three cabins Alan had built around a waterfall. These modest structures were but a foothold for the master plan he has since executed with his trademark patience and perfectionism over two decades. After spending years studying the property's topography, views, and nature, he erected his home on an elevated site overlooking verdant fields and the Catskills across the river from Columbia County. In an adjacent forest stands his studio, clad in dark wood that melds into its sylvan surroundings. Having photographed many of his projects for shelter magazines and the 2013 monograph *Journey: The Life and Times of an American Architect*, I've witnessed the way Alan designs in concert with the landscape to encourage a deep connection with the world itself. It's an imperative he puts into practice not only for himself and his clients but also in support of students as a member of the board of trustees at Parsons and president of the board of trustees at the Skowhegan School of Painting and Sculpture—a position he vacated at the end of 2022 after two terms. He's also an avid supporter of Housing Works, his firm having designed the organization's first building, Cylar House, in the East Village. When one passes through the front door of their home, it's not the interior that first impresses, but the idyllic terrain seen through the wall of windows. As your eyes adjust, a signature Wanzenberg scene emerges: a low center of gravity recalling mid-century California design, choice woods exquisitely milled, art and furniture in earthy tones, forms by masters of their craft like Ruth Asawa and Mario Dal Fabbro, and inset bookcases that would be the envy of any bibliophile. For all of his possessions, it is his two dachshunds and vast library that Alan cherishes most. When he showed me a small volume by Richard Neutra inscribed to fellow architect Albert Frey, it became a holy object in his hands. Alan lives by the motto of the YMCA: mind, body, and spirit. He reads widely, swims daily, and practices his trade with the spiritual intention of a monk or a craftsman of an earlier era. Besides meticulous millwork and joinery, color is a thread that connects his disparate projects, from Costa Rica to the Hudson Valley and far beyond. The inner walls of the cabins, for example, are painted a deep red that would please Matisse. From picking paints, to learning piano, to cultivating bonsai trees, Alan takes his time to get it right, and as anyone lucky enough to pass through his projects knows, right is worth the wait.

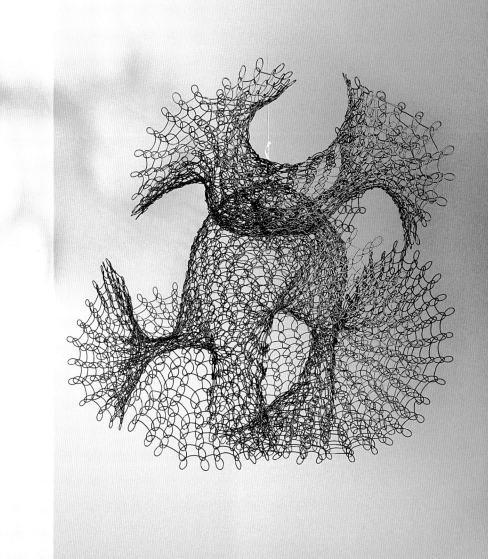

MELORA KUHN

Drive two hours due north from Manhattan and you'll find Germantown, a little cradle of art and history and art history hugging the east bank of the waterway called Mahicannituck—the river that flows two ways—by the Native Americans who once occupied the Hudson River's shores. Your trip will roughly parallel that taken by the 1,200 Palatine German refugees for whom the region is named, settled here by Anne, Queen of Great Britain and Ireland, in 1710. Today, Germantown is a refuge for creatives who, consciously or not, follow in the footsteps of Frederic Church, the nineteenth-century landscape painter who lived and worked nearby (see pages 112–23). True to this landscape, history and myth pulse through the work and home of renowned artist Melora Kuhn. Her historic farmstead is a clear extension of her canvases and sculptures, possessing the same sense of fairytale and imagination. Its rooms are grounded by old wooden floors and uplifted by walls painted white and tender shades of blue. Some surfaces are left exquisitely raw: wallpaper peeling in perfect little ringlets suggest there's something unseen beneath

the surface, a theme Melora often mines in her work. The day I visited, the red barn that houses her studio was framed by a fresh coat of snow. Inside, Melora was halfway through a portrait of a young woman in nineteenth-century dress, facial tattoos descending unexpectedly from her lower lip to her chin. Melora later told me that her mysterious subject was one Olive Oatman, captured by Native Americans in 1851, when she was thirteen, and ransomed back into white society six years later, ink and all. Behind the artist, stretching from wall to wall in her workspace, was an enormous canvas. Upon it, an exotic panorama, looking in its unfinished state like the hand-painted wallpapers a Livingston might have installed in a manor house nearby. Small figures, portraits, vitrines, busts, photographs, postcards, books, taxidermy, and found objects proliferate, but never descend into clutter. There's an inscrutable logic to Melora's universe, a steady, searching thread that connects her work, life, and dwelling. It's all a bit mysterious, the kind of mystery that draws you closer and closer to the canvas until you disappear, forgetting another world exists outside.

GARY TINTEROW ✛ CHRISTOPHER GARDNER

If history is in the wallpaper, the Wynkoop House tells quite a tale. Built for Cornelius Wynkoop, a wealthy merchant from a Dutch line that settled these parts in the 1680s, the stone structure predates America's founding by four years. Its gambrel roof is drawn from traditional Dutch architecture, while the Georgian plan is plainly English, a rare mix of influences representing the two primary powers that colonized this region in the wee hours before the dawn of the American project. One winter night in 1782, one of the fathers of that project, George Washington, slept in a room on the second floor. His ghost lingers: our first president still gazes from lithographs, paintings, and sculptures throughout the house. Gary Tinterow, director of the Museum of Fine Arts, Houston, and his husband, Christopher Gardner, an antiques dealer, now occupy Wynkoop.

In their care, it has changed very little since Washington's visit: a specimen of history preserved in amber. Paint clinging to the woodwork dates to the early nineteenth century (at least), pine floors remain unsealed and unvarnished, Delft tiles with biblical scenes flank the fireplace, original plasterwork clouds the walls, and period-correct finishes are relied on for repairs. The uncanny patina of this place has made Wynkoop and its magnificent boxwood parterre garden a beloved backdrop for productions over the years. I've shot many of them. Inside, it is a photographer's playground: oversized restoration-glass windows filter rippled light in unpredictable, painterly ways. I find that the older the home, the more stories it tells. My goal is to record those stories—some real, some imagined—as printed impressions of light and color on the page.

EXO:32

MAT:

RON SHARKEY

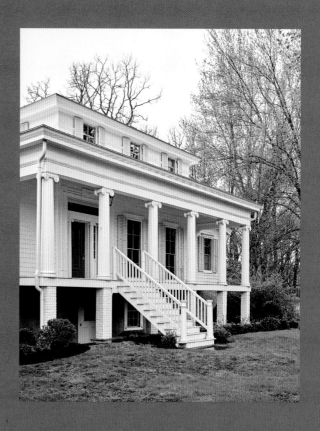

I met Maple Lawn in the rain. Fronted by six Ionic columns, this stately Greek Revival home sits on Main Street in historic Stone Ridge, next door to the Wynkoop House (see pages 46–59). Constructed as a residence and workplace for Dr. Jacob Louis Hasbrouck in 1843, Maple Lawn is the purest illustration of classical style in the hamlet, its plan likely adopted from an 1835 book by the influential American architect Minard Lafever. Despite its august history, antiques dealer Ron Sharkey saw the structure as a clean slate: an opportunity to engineer a new way of living after parting with his previous home in nearby Accord. Whereas his Accord house was isolated down a long dirt road and furnished in a rambling English style, Maple Lawn is situated on a bustling thoroughfare (by upstate standards) and refreshingly airy, with the aesthetic restraint of a Swedish farmhouse. Its rarefied atmosphere is the result of a painstaking multi-year renovation that burned through no less than four contractors as floors were raised and lowered, leaky gutters replaced, and walls moved wholesale. Throughout, Sharkey was careful to preserve Maple Lawn's old soul, with smoky discoloration left tinting the painted brick above a fireplace and exposed stone walls a steadfast reminder of centuries past. Maple Lawn seemed to glow even on a dark day, with light pouring through the generous windows and delineating the grain of rustic wooden tabletops, ironstone ceramics, and antique ticking fabric. And

though the palette skews pale, Maple Lawn is no monochrome monolith. Darker corners surprise and entice, like the moody gray parlor with its original black-and-gold marble mantel. Born in New Jersey, Sharkey is dashing and energetic, smartly dressed on the day we met in a crisp Levi's jacket, gold corduroys, and blue-tinted eyeglasses, more cosmopolitan creative director than country shopkeeper. Friends have frequently visited since he settled into the new house. Photographers like me have approached him to shoot it repeatedly. I was, therefore, merely one of many moths drawn to Maple Lawn's lantern, seeking the warmth between its walls in a dark season.

MARK McDONALD ✛ DWAYNE RESNICK

When I began discussing this project with friends in the Catskills and Hudson Valley, the names Mark McDonald and Dwayne Resnick kept coming up. The January day I visited their home, Japanese maple and cherry trees peeked through a blanket of snow, evidence that the property is designed to shine in all seasons. Resnick is a yogi, and McDonald a pioneering dealer of mid-century furniture, art, and jewelry. Naturally, the home is a trove of museum-quality gems: television stands and side tables by Frank Lloyd Wright; a black leather Eames chair; Calder mobiles; vessels by Gunnar Nylund and Berndt Friberg; a balloon-like chandelier by Naho Lino. Works by young ceramists—including a colorful teapot by Roberto Lugo with Notorious B.I.G.'s likeness—grace various surfaces, books congregate in low stacks, and a hulking stone fireplace anchors the interior's naturalist palette of light wood, patinated leather, and rich red velvet.

A long-haired Weimaraner, that breed of ghostly appearance and fierce intelligence, lazed in the pale light while I photographed. I love documenting the personal collection of a professional collector, taking note of the items someone so immersed in aesthetics chooses to live with, like the ocular tiles by artist Stephen Knapp that gaze over the tub in the primary bathroom, sourced from the exterior of New York's beloved but now defunct Alexander's department store. I'm struck not only by curation itself, but by how the connoisseur gathers certain objects together, as if in conversation. Glass shelves in the library support objets d'art with no purpose but to please, lit from above like a display in some museum of anthropology. Defying the clean lines and austerity most of us (dubiously) associate with mid-century design, this living space exudes energy and color, a warm reprieve from the monochrome expanse of ice and skeletal forest outside.

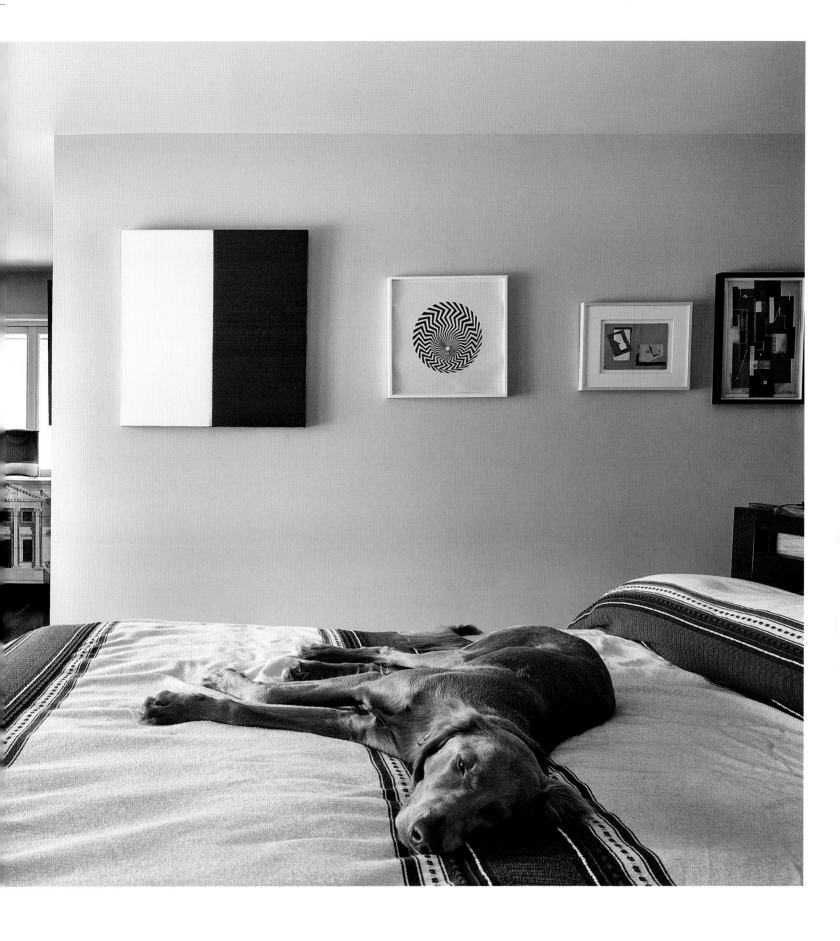

PETER FRANK ✝ JONATHAN LERNER

My old friend Peter Frank is the founder of Friends of Hudson Youth and a (retired) stylist and set designer with whom I've collaborated on countless shoots and projects over the past quarter century. His husband, Jonathan Lerner, is a writer on issues of landscape and architecture, and the author of multiple novels and an extraordinary memoir of his days as "minister of propaganda" for the Weathermen—of the militant, not meteorological, variety—titled *Swords in the Hands of Children.* Their immaculately restored home in Hudson, built in 1870, is painted the color of deep red clay, and the façade stunningly captures the afternoon light. Entering the front door and mudroom at the foot of the stairs, visitors are met with wicker baskets, canes, market bags, and straw hats, as if you're entering the home of an eccentric English country squire. The wooden floors are painted a glossy light gray throughout, like the solemn sky in a painting from the Dutch Golden Age. Paired with natural wood tones, tapestries, woven rugs, worn leather, and subtle reddish echoes of the exterior, the place has a subdued atmosphere. It is a thinker's place, reflecting Peter's keen eye and Jonathan's curious mind. Framed photographs and works in charcoal, pencil, and paint hang salon-style, making effortless little vignettes. Bookshelves are weighted with the couple's eclectic collections, including beautiful antique volumes by Ludwig Bemelmans and Oscar Wilde. For me, the focal point is the portrait of Peter by Brenda Zlamany, his eyes intently gazing out from the canvas. Painted in a classical, chiaroscuro style, he resembles a medieval scholar illuminated by firelight. Appropriately so. There is a deep intelligence and warmth within these walls, conjuring a pure devotion to craft, learning, and humanity.

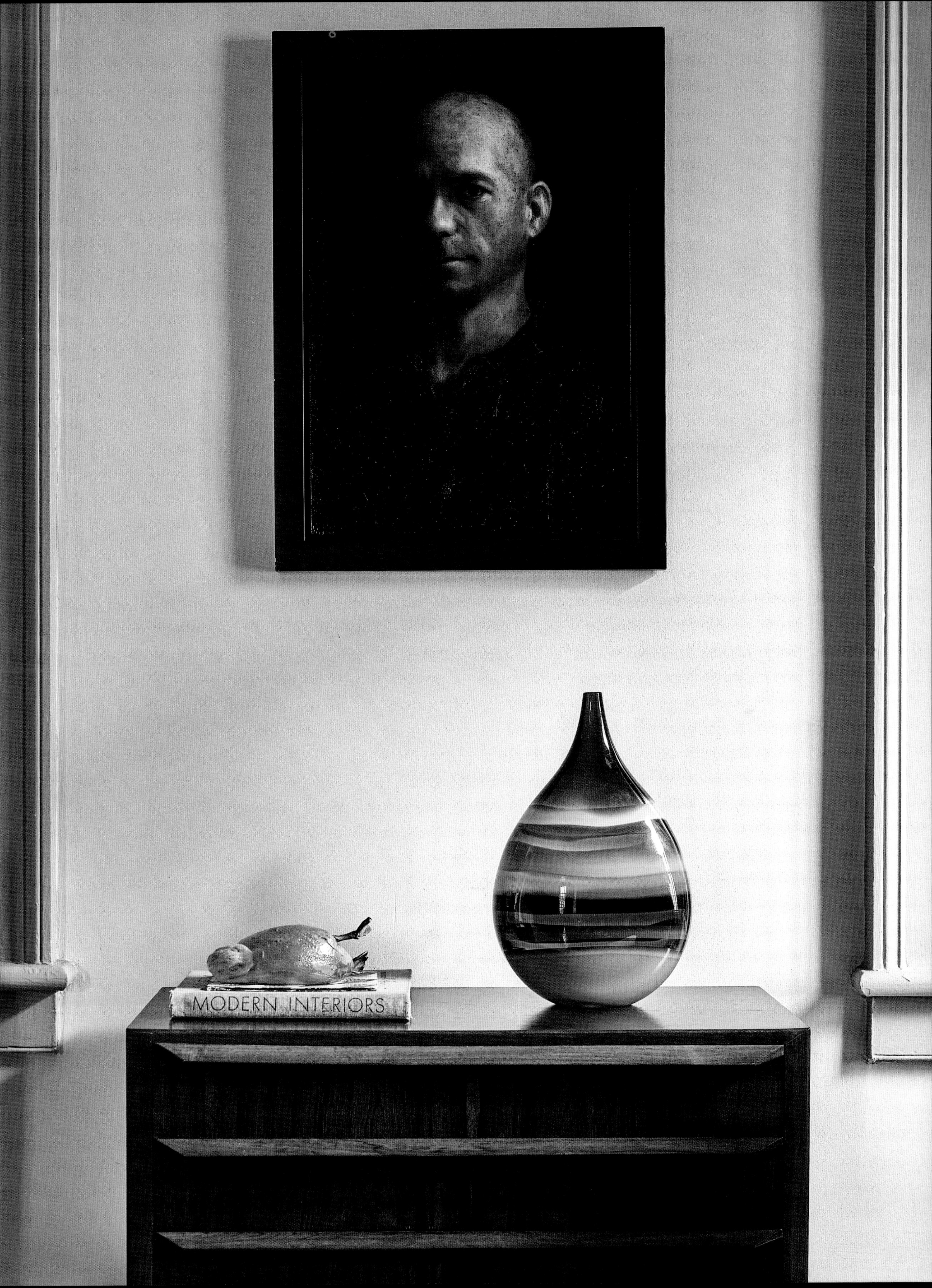
MODERN INTERIORS

MARIA + THOMAS COLE

Thomas Cole is the quintessential artist of the Hudson River School, and this is an artist's house. Perched in Catskill overlooking Cole's beloved "blue mountains" to the west and the Hudson River to the east, the farm known as Cedar Grove served as the painter's studio and residence from 1836 until his death in 1848. Cole was a pioneering American landscape artist, documenting the undeveloped expanses of our Northeast with sweeping views of its mountains, valleys, and creeks; skies pregnant with storm clouds; and subtle characters—picnickers, sportsmen, Mohicans—dwarfed by the worlds they occupy. These were not just pretty pictures, but powerful statements in defiance of Andrew Jackson's destructive environmental policies. Cole's paintings, along with the works of fellow elite artists of the Jacksonian era, were instrumental in mobilizing the federal government to take conservation seriously and are considered a catalyst for the creation of the national parks system. The stool that once supported Cole now rests beside an easel in his studio, as if the artist rose one day to stretch his legs and never returned. A monogrammed trunk ("TC") and the collected works of Byron reinforce the image of a man on the move. Appropriate for this astute observer of nature, the outdoors bleed into Cedar Grove in wonderful ways, with painted walls of periwinkle and terra-cotta, shells and starfish, floral tiles and carpets, and layers of pattern on pattern recalling the tangled forests Cole explored with pad and pencil. His method of sketching *en plein air* before committing romanticized visions to canvas back at his studio drew an entire movement of artists into the hills, notably Frederic Church, whose home is situated just across the Hudson in poetic symmetry of master and student (see pages 112–23). Cole wasn't the only accomplished artist in the family: his sister Sarah's paintings grace the walls as well. Stare into Thomas Cole's works and you become drunk on the majesty of untapped wilderness. His home has a similar effect, a monument to unmitigated kinship with nature.

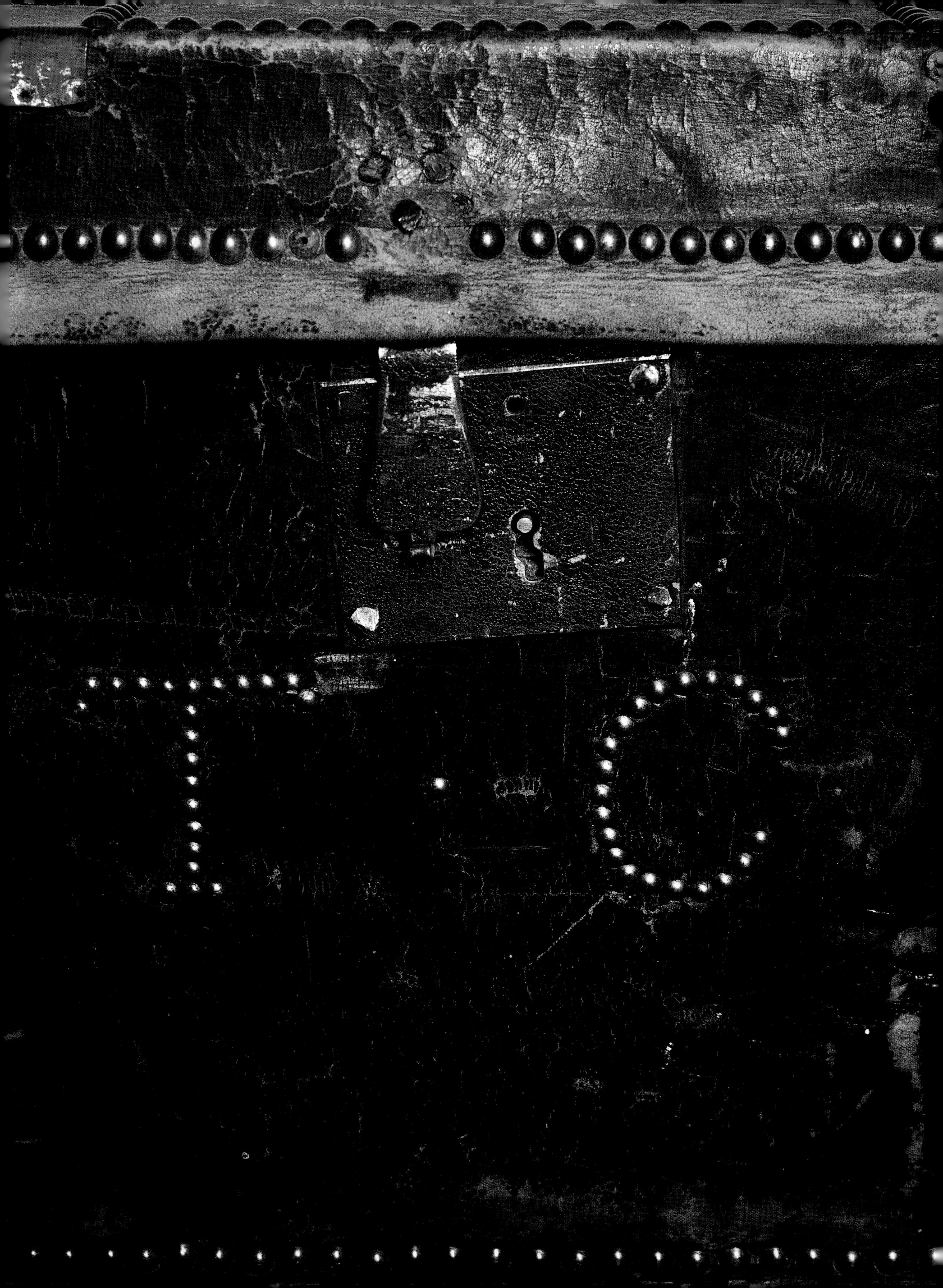

ISABEL + FREDERIC CHURCH

In 1869, Frederic and Isabel Church returned to their Hudson Valley farm after an eighteen-month grand tour of Europe and the Middle East. As the foremost member of the second generation of Hudson River School painters, a creative lineage founded by his mentor, Thomas Cole (see pages 98–111), Frederic was one of the most famous artists in America. Despite their long voyage, the couple was restless, eager to raise a new home on their property, which Church had acquired in 1860 and would expand over the following decades to encompass a sprawling 250-acre experiment in agriculture, landscape design, architecture, and conservation. Drawing on the built wonders they'd encountered in Beirut, Jerusalem, and Damascus, the couple tapped Calvert Vaux, co-creator of Central Park, to help them design a singular structure that merged Eastern and Western motifs. The house that resulted from this eccentric marriage, called Olana, is like a mirage: a Persian-style mansion with Victorian elements on a hilltop looming above the river, with a hawk's-eye view of the Catskills, Taconic Mountains, and the dramatic play of cloud and sun that continuously refashions the valley. Church managed the details with the obsessive attention of a fine artist, drafting architectural sketches, designing ornamental stencils, framing sightlines, and filling the house with furniture, art, and objects accumulated on his travels. He even mixed the iconic ocher color scheme on his own well-worn palette. Most important, Olana was Church's opportunity to magnify his skill in rendering romantic views of nature far beyond

the scale of any canvas. Rivers were the primary arteries of commerce in the nineteenth century, and as industry pushed inland, the forests around the Hudson had been razed with abandon. Church energetically reforested his property with native seeds and saplings: maple, birch, hickory, hemlock, oak, and more. But this was no mere remediation. He used planting (and other forms of landscaping) as a form of painting, molding his world to his fancy by framing some views, obscuring others, masking structures, and insulating the carriage roads that circulated workers and guests across the estate. In a letter sent during construction, Church put it bluntly: "I have made about 1¾ miles of road this season, opening entirely new and beautiful views. I can make more and better landscapes in this way than by tampering with canvas and paint in the studio." As a repository of Church's creative vision, this spectacular "viewshed" is as vital as the house itself, and since Olana was saved from destruction in 1966, a passionate union of public and private forces has largely succeeded in preserving the landscape seen from her grounds through a combination of acquisition and easement. In its work, this alliance between groups like Scenic Hudson, Open Space Institute, Audubon New York, and The Olana Partnership continues Church's mission to protect the region from industrialization and deforestation—then, as now, threatening America's once seemingly infinite but all-too-finite wilderness. As a result, Olana towers even above Church's beloved paintings as the artist's most enduring and beguiling masterpiece.

DOUG + MIKE STARN

Stepping into the warehouse studio of Doug and Mike Starn in Beacon, New York, is like entering a cathedral. There is the sheer scale of the 40,000-square-foot space, once used as a foundry for casting patriotic monuments and sculptures by luminaries like Louise Bourgeois and Jeff Koons. And then there is the dizzying abundance of contents, the most striking of which is an immense floating cloud of bamboo poles held together by colorful tape. Suspended within, like insects caught in sap, are a dozen or so harnessed climbers deconstructing and reconstructing the fixture pole by pole. Through their antlike efforts, the installation migrates very slowly from one side of the warehouse to another, epitomizing the brothers' lauded mixture of art and performance. These identical twins—inseparable collaborators and art world legends—are far from New Jersey, where they were born in 1961 and started making art together around the kitchen table as kids, much like my own sons, not twins but as close as brothers can be. It seems they've merely magnified their childhood kitchen table to titanic proportions, to the delight of the millions who have witnessed and interacted with their creations at locations ranging from the U.S. Embassy in Moscow to the Japanese island of Naoshima. Notably, their 2010 rooftop installation at the Metropolitan Museum drew more than 600,000 visitors over six months, making it one of the museum's most popular exhibitions of all time. I became aware of the Starns in the late

1980s, when they still were primarily associated with photography, producing works that mined the depths of light and dark through an innocent and wondrous lens in arresting series like *Blot Out the Sun* and *Absorption of Light*. The essayist Demetrio Paparoni summarized my impressions perfectly in the Starns' book *Attracted to Light*: "For the Starns, light is more than enlightenment; it is the gravity of all our past experiences and our future, the conscious and the unconscious, the external and internal factors that drive our lives." For me, as a fellow photographer, their sacred conception of our medium's essential element resonated deeply, so I savored the chance to meet the artists, visit their workspace, and document their ingenuity in progress.

GEOFF HOWELL

When Geoff Howell, the owner and creative director of a 3D design and build company, started restoring and renovating his home in 2004, one might assume he looked to the history of its original inhabitants for inspiration. Edward Van Loon, who built the Italianate structure in 1866, bore the name of a storied Dutch family tracing its lineage to the first Europeans to settle this riverside region, today called Athens. Instead, Howell looked to poignant recollections of his own family and upbringing in Washington, New Jersey. He traces his interest in historic architecture to visiting a neighbor's eighteenth-century home, which stood in stark contrast to the Formica-clad, fluorescent-lit home of his grandmother. He was transfixed by the details and their sense of time: wood floors and walls, an old cooking stove, Edison bulbs, Blue Willow dishware. Howell's mother would tell stories about the prosperity of their extended family before the Great Depression, inspiring Howell to effectively re-create, years later, what a multi-generational family home might have looked like had history gone differently. Removing asbestos siding and asphalt roofing, adding a terrace, pond, and plant room, and restoring two bathrooms and the kitchen allowed the home's historic character to re-emerge. Selecting American and English antique ornaments, furnishings, and materials in the course of his nose-to-tail refresh, Howell dedicated several rooms to particular people in his life: his mother, great-aunt, and great-grandmother, all of whom loved nineteenth-century European porcelain and decorative arts. Another honors his grandmother, a woman of deep faith who served as the organist and choirmaster at their parish church for twenty-five years. On the wall are enlarged holy cards like those distributed by churches to honor a particular saint in prayer. (The odd Eastern Orthodox icon sneaks in to stir things up.) Beneath the gaze of saints and mothers and messiahs, we bonded over our common Catholic upbringings, laughing about being subjected to *Our Lady of Perpetual Pain*, as I used to jokingly call the Marian sculpture that lorded over my school. Having carefully furnished every conceivable corner of the house, Howell is now turning his attention to the gardens and grounds, planting catalpas, dawn redwoods, oaks, and maples in a characteristically maximalist yet deliberate scheme. Inside and out, such abundance would spell chaos in the hands of a lesser aesthete. But Howell is a man with a plan, guided by the memories that make his old house a magnificent shrine to things (and people) past.

KATHRYN ✝
SIMONE SCOTT

Architect and designer Kathryn Scott was first drawn to Rhinebeck by the tale of a mansion in ruin. Built in 1853 by Manhattan socialite Elizabeth Schermerhorn Jones, a relative of the Astors and aunt to Edith Wharton, Wyndcliffe Mansion inspired Jones's peers to erect increasingly ambitious homes along the Hudson. (This is apparently the origin of the phrase "keeping up with the Joneses.") The estate was abandoned in 1950, and ever since has been melting gradually into the encroaching wilderness. The notion that nature subdues all human works (and vanities) is reflected beautifully in all of Kathryn's projects, many of which I photographed

for her 2018 monograph, *Creating Beauty.* The same principle holds for the Rhinebeck residence Kathryn now occupies with her daughter, Simone. She purchased the stately red-brick structure, built in 2002 to resemble a traditional carriage house, in 2004, and set about shaping the gardens and landscape surrounding it. The house stands dignified and quite vertical atop a rise overlooking the Hudson Valley and endless hills wrinkling away to the distant Berkshires. A trio of nests on the mantel and the husk of a wasp's nest on the table invite the idea that Kathryn finds inspiration in the ingenuity of animal dwellings. Logs stacked in a long, sinuous line were installed as an art piece, making use of fallen timber collected during the clearance of the plot. Wild meadows of grass and fern kissed by wind and insects and birds fan out in every direction toward towering forest, mediated by a buffer of lush vegetable and flower gardens. Vast windows make the place glow like a lighthouse, illuminating the magnificently complex grain of the predominantly dark wooden surfaces and breathing life into the smoky-blue paint coating the dining room walls. Objects laden with meaning occupy the interior, including prototypes by Kathryn herself: a coffee table based on ancient terra-cotta tomb slabs, a two-drawer chest, and delicate porcelain vessels. Inspired by the Gilded Age estates of Newport, where even the minutest details, down to light switches and handles, were custom made by craftspeople, Kathryn installed antique hardware throughout the house. The solar array that powers it has its own (unexpected) sculptural beauty, like something out of Storm King, the land-art mecca on the other side of the river. If an architect's own home is the purest reflection of their values and aesthetics, it's clear Kathryn sees nature as an artist without equal.

JESSICA PIAZZA ✛ TIM UNICH

The Catskills are a study in contrasts. The winters are long, cold, and dark. The summers are brief, warm, and beautiful. There's a certain intensity of green that arrives each spring, and every year it comes as a surprise. How can this barren landscape unlock such life? And in winter, conversely, how can this Eden simply vanish? The Saugerties home of Jessica Piazza and Tim Unich possesses a similar quality, manipulating light and dark in a way that isn't so much disorienting as intoxicating. When I visited in early June, that hallucinatory green framed my entrance down a long gravel road. Their lovingly restored antique house sits on a rounded pedestal, carpeted all around by meadow encircled by forest. Well behind the house stands an exposed wall of the earth's crust—a vein of cracked bluestone—evidence of an old quarry that once contributed to the construction of Manhattan's sidewalks in the days before concrete. The residence is painted gray, echoing this distinctive geology, one of countless points of communication with nature throughout the property. Bee boxes, an ambitious garden, and a greenhouse bespeak a family nourished by the land, underscored by the Hunter boots, wicker baskets, and bee suits at hand in the mudroom. Against the house's traditional and somewhat austere exterior, a bright red door hints that there's something unexpected within. The living room is lined with dense nautical wallpaper bearing all manner of fish, anemones, and aquatic flora, rendered in the style of German artist-zoologist Ernst Haeckel. This first struck me as a non sequitur—sea creatures in the mountains?—until I remembered that millions of years ago, the area where the Catskills now sprawl was submerged beneath a shallow sea. Densely layered rooms like this give way to open, soaring, loft-like spaces, epitomized by an expansive kitchen with marble countertops, a wood-fire oven, and a Lacanche range from France. Reflecting this region of contradictions, the lights feel lighter and the darks darker in this home. Whether it's those brutal winters or the isolation enforced by such rugged topography, upstate living can take on a certain survivalist strain: chopping wood, prepping for blizzards, growing food. In the event of an apocalypse, you could do worse than find your way to Piazza and Unich's pastoral compound: just follow the red door through the trees.

MITA + GERALD BLAND

books and croquet mallets and firewood and dogs mingle organically, like free-range chickens. Mita's watercolors coat the walls, accompanied by sporting art, architectural prints, old photographs, and the odd modern piece, armoring every surface in carefree agglomerations. Gerald's trade cycles furniture in and out in a continuous game of interior Tetris. The morning I visited, a gilt frame reclined on the floor; by noon it was fitted with a distressed antique mirror, ready for a prestigious place on a mantel somewhere. Chairs with age-worn upholstery—pieces that less discerning hands might discard—add to the prevailing air of comfort, making for inviting places to rest after a long stroll around the grounds. Gerald played the part of country host par excellence, always orbited by a scrambling pack of spaniels and Yorkies. For lunch he served pot pie on a bed of leafy greens, drizzled with olive oil from Mita's family farm in Tuscany, plus a precious dab of molasses-thick balsamic from Modena. As the light faded, I packed my camera and said farewell to Diogenes, convinced that sometimes it's just fine to dwell in the past.

The face of Diogenes welcomed me like a sentry as I approached the Stanfordville home of Mita and Gerald Bland. His stone bust stands on a tidy stone wall overlooking the lawn: an upgrade for the ancient Cynic philosopher known to sleep in large ceramic jars in the agora of Athens. History runs deep here. Gerald is an antiquarian, Mita an artist. The original house was built in 1767, the later Greek Revival wing in 1840. It sits on a hearty seventy-eight acres down a narrow dirt road just a stone's throw from the Hudson, and like a proper Hudson Valley country manor, the atmosphere inside is one of controlled chaos. Boots and

JENNIFER McLAWHORN ☩ CHRISTOPHER KISSOCK

Driving from our home in Margaretville to visit our friends Jen McLawhorn and Chris Kissock means snaking along the Pepacton Reservoir before passing south into the Beaverkill Valley. As the topography softens, cradling its namesake river (*kill* means "body of water" in Dutch) toward the Delaware, we enter a storied landscape peopled by seekers of all stripes living tucked away in discreet hollows formed by the famous waterway's many tributaries. The trout-filled Beaverkill is known as the birthplace of fly-fishing in this country, but it is also in many ways a headwater of our modern environmental movement. In 1970, activists, including local resident John Adams, formed the Natural Resources Defense Council, or NRDC, which has become our nation's foremost defender of clean land, air, and water. Today, a new generation of settlers, including Jen and Chris, is following earlier sportsmen and conservation-minded landowners into the valley, and finding a warm welcome. Up a steep bank from an offspring of the Beaverkill called Berry Brook is their impressive lodge of glass, maple, and pine partly cantilevered over the slope. The "Cliff House," as architect Marlys Hann called it, was built in 1998 for two fixtures of this tight-knit local community with the intention of keeping the property and its surroundings wild. Jen, a casting director, and Chris, a partner at a respected Brooklyn creative agency, have proudly inherited the space and the spirit in which it was created. The community has adopted them with open arms, perhaps sensing their dedication to continuing the valley's tradition of living quietly and close to the land. Jen spends her free hours foraging and making arrangements from flora sourced from the hillside. Chris is an avid hiker, skier, fisherman, and cyclist involved in the recent rejuvenation of the

Catskill Art Space in nearby Livingston Manor. While weighing furnishings and improvements, they consult the original blueprints to discern the architect's intent, prioritizing the revival of objects left by the previous inhabitants—like a set of paper lanterns restored with help from the Noguchi Museum—over new introductions. Beyond the soothing tone of timber, worked everywhere into soaring configurations that recall Frank Lloyd Wright, the palette is disciplined, indebted to Nordic and East Asian traditions. The sense of quiet is profound, but crack one of the ample windows and the sound of water and wind through the hemlocks fills the room. Like the nearby brook that feeds the Beaverkill, which feeds the Delaware, Jen and Chris are, in their simple way, bringing new energy to something bigger than themselves. In a world that often spurns the past for the present, they're proving continuity can be more radical than reinvention.

ROGER ROSS WILLIAMS + CASPER DE BOER

In the 1870s, a Union veteran moved back to his family plot in the central Catskills town of Roxbury. Having become prosperous as a Mississippi steamboat captain after the Civil War, he constructed a grand house in the center hall Colonial style, with some Southern flourishes he likely picked up on his travels. Among them is a wrought-iron widow's walk that gave the place a vaguely maritime feel, despite the fact that it overlooks pine-cloaked mountains, not white-tipped waves. Over more than a century, the house passed through many hands, finally landing in the possession of Roger Ross Williams, a celebrated filmmaker with the astonishing distinction of being the first African American director to win an Academy Award for his 2010 film, *Music by Prudence*. He was later joined by his husband, Casper de Boer, an actor with credits including the 1986 Dutch film *The Assault*, which took home both the Academy Award and the Golden Globe for Best Foreign Language Film. They transformed the estate into a beloved event venue, with de Boer now expertly directing events and shaping the fifty-acre property

into a dreamscape for picturesque weddings hosting up to 140 people. Williams admitted candidly to me that when he first moved to the area, there were few openly gay people around, and even fewer Blacks. It still isn't uncommon to see Confederate flags in the Catskills, and for an artist whose work often deals with questions of inclusivity (such as his 2013 film *God Loves Uganda*, which explores the influence of American Evangelical missionary activity on the denial of LGBTQ+ rights in Africa), historical memory (his upcoming adaptation of *The 1619 Project*), and Black culture (his 2019 documentary *The Apollo* tells the story of the legendary venue), Williams understands the weight of his presence in this house, property, and region. He told me that he sees the house as a "testament to resilience," and in that spirit, the couple's style is quietly triumphant, from the way the house seems to soak up light to the Oscar and Golden Globe trophies on a beat-up filing cabinet in one corner. There are indications of a searching curiosity, like the well-appointed library filled with books by authors ranging from Victor Hugo to Toni Morrison, and the coffee table cluttered with volumes by Barack Obama, Ibram X. Kendi, and Ta-Nehisi Coates. And then there are instances of real tenderness, like the urn containing the ashes of Roger's mother on a shelf, and the two childhood portraits of de Boer and Williams in small oval frames above their bed. Every detail is drawn out by that vivid Catskills light; even darker rooms, like the library, painted charcoal, were luminous on the gray day I visited. Today, some 150 years after its construction by a Mississippi steamboat captain, new captains inhabit this grand estate, navigators of uncharted cultural waters, steering our ship toward a more open, honest, and hopeful horizon.

ANDREA MENKE ✝ CLARK SANDERS

Even before Rip Van Winkle dozed off in the mountains above his village and woke up two decades later, the Hudson Valley has generated tales of the mystic. Maybe it's the riddle of the landscape, the way it at once obscures and lures. An invitation to the East Meredith home of Andrea Menke and Clark Sanders is an invitation into the mystic. It starts with the drive, which takes you up gentle rises and through idyllic farm-studded valleys. Built with wood and stone scavenged from crumbled walls and topped by a vertiginous steeple, the structure epitomizes Clark's belief that a house is a livable sculpture. He started constructing it in the northern Catskills town when he was only nineteen. The stonework alone took a decade, with the final slates set in the roof twenty-five years after breaking ground. His life's work is, at first glance, rooted in the architecture of old Europe. But on deeper inspection it reveals a promiscuous range of influences, registering somewhere between a pagoda and a château, with a dose of Gaudí and a dash of hobbit. I was amazed by the living room, with its smooth stone floor underfoot, hand-hewn beech mantel, gracefully milled pine ceiling boards and beams of ash, maple, and white oak, and boulder set into the floor. Overhead, a bridge built of a single cherry plank harvested from a tree by their driveway links an upstairs common space and a bedroom, just one of the whimsical details that permeate the house and sixty-four-acre property. Another is the clawfoot iron tub that sits atop a shed, where Andrea bathes amid the hemlocks in the summer. Ever since I've known her, Andrea has marched to the beat of her own drum, rolling up to the shoots where we first met in a restored orange VW bus. Her shop in Delhi, The Stonehouse, is a storybook sliver of space selling home goods sourced from markets around the world. In the house, every surface is beautifully styled with those skillful finds, from Indian fabrics over the beds to Moroccan rugs hanging from the banister like medieval tapestries. The presence of flora and fauna in every direction adds to the earthy feel: cats sleeping in stone niches built for that very purpose; flowers blooming in the gardens Andrea has cultivated; her miniature donkeys, a gift from Clark, milling about lazily in a nearby field; chickens pecking in the grass. Driving away, I felt a little like Rip, thrust back into the world after a fantastical dream.

JOHN MARKUS

Standing at his coveted Franklin smoker to monitor a sizzling pork butt, John Markus can survey 180 degrees of rolling hills and farmland fanning out from his 854-acre property. He jokes that he wants to be able to see when "they" come for him. Comedy and cooking are entwined in John, a writer, producer, director, and playwright with credits including *Taxi*, *The Cosby Show*, *A Different World*, and *The Larry Sanders Show*. When his friend and writing partner Al Franken served him a batch of bad ribs at dinner one night, it sparked his competitive curiosity and drew him deep into the arena of Southern barbecue. His trial by fire included training under top-brass pitmasters from Kansas City to Alabama, producing the reality TV show *BBQ Pitmasters*, and directing the short film *The Kings of BBQ Barbeque Kuwait*, about smoking meats for troops overseas. I wouldn't venture a guess about which accolade means more to him: his Emmy or his induction into the Barbecue Hall of

Fame. He tells me he likes to write in his head while cooking. It makes sense. Barbecue and writing both require time, patience, restraint, and the humility to endure cycles of trial and error. From the stone patio outside his home, I watch smoke float over the meadows that extend in every direction, garnished with a galaxy of white wildflowers. Behind me is the house, an impressive structure by my friend Alan Wanzenberg, whose own house is featured on pages 18–31. It respects its surroundings on a gentle rise, with large windows that are conduits for floods of light and a spacious screened porch that must often feature the intoxicating scents of John's smoker and cigars. The interiors, also by Wanzenberg, bear all the hallmarks of his masterful manipulation of wood and stone in the service of serene, restrained spaces. The furnishings, many designed by Wanzenberg himself, lend an added sense of lightness: tables the color of chlorophyll, armchairs clothed in rich saffron-hued fabrics, red velvet cushions, dark green cabinetry. On one wall, two avian portraits by the painter Walton Ford and a third by John James Audubon roost quietly. I was especially drawn to the study, its barrel-vaulted ceiling of dark cedar vaguely recalling the interior of a ship—a nod to Markus's immigrant parents. A daybed nestled into an alcove looks like the perfect place to doze off between drafts. It is a craftsman's house, a writer's house, a chef's house, designed to slow time in pursuit of the well-chosen word—or the perfectly seasoned cut of pork.

JASON FRANK ✞ VINNY LOPEZ

Lopez. It seems appropriate that Jason, creative lead at Ralph Lauren Home, and Vinny, a writer, landed here, in one of the oldest homes in Andes, on a plot once settled by a soldier of the Revolution. Both Jason and Vinny are keen students of history, and, having met Jason while photographing for Ralph Lauren, I've always been impressed by his ability to conjure the feel of an older America from object, placement, texture, and composition—an integral aspect of the brand's timeless allure. As stewards of this property, they consider themselves not remodelers but researchers, drawing on hints from history for inspiration. When they moved in, neighbors and descendants of the area's old farming families knocked on their door with photos and illustrations. The home even appears in a quaint illustration in W. W. Munsell's *History of Delaware County*, published in 1880. From the exterior, it hasn't changed much in the intervening centuries. Inside, the couple peeled back layers of "suburbanization" from the 1970s and '80s—mauve carpets, vinyl siding—to reveal elements long dormant underneath. Vinny told me: "It's like it had just been sleeping, and instead of restoration, it was like we'd woken it back up." Splashed effortlessly across this fresh slate is their collection of Americana and antiques, everything seeming to possess the type of authentic patina money can't buy. Throughout the property, they unearthed old stone walls, farm equipment, and stoves abandoned by the stream, each discovery adding a new degree of clarity to their picture of the past. From the days when Native Americans, revolutionary fugitives, up-renters, and down-renters haunted these hills, to the fleeting present, this place has witnessed history unfold, and in Jason and Vinny's hands, that story is far from finished.

In the balmy August of 1845, a hotheaded undersheriff named Osman Steele rode out to the farm of Moses Earle, a sixty-four-year-old tenant refusing to pay $64 in rent to his landlord, Charlotte Verplanck. Earle's small resistance situated the farmer within a regional uprising against the feudal system that then governed upstate New York, a historical footnote known as the "Anti-Rent War." Starting in 1839, tax collectors and their allies had been eluded, harassed, tarred, and feathered across the Catskills, often at the hands of menacing bands of armed farmers disguised in the spirit of the Boston Tea Party "Indians." Home-made sheepskin masks hid their identity, and they wore overshirts and trousers sewn from local calico, hence their name: "Calico Indians." Perhaps emboldened by strong drink at the Hunting Tavern in the village of Andes, Steele was determined to auction Earle's livestock to compensate for the late pay. But when he arrived at the pasture, he was met by more than two hundred masked "down-renters" determined to block the sale. In the tense standoff that ensued, Steele was struck by a bullet; his body was borne through the hills to the same tavern where he'd been drinking (and reportedly boasted of his invincibility) only hours earlier. On the way, the solemn procession passed the quiet Colonial farmhouse today occupied by Jason Frank and Vinny

HANNAH LEIGHTON ✠ CHRISTIAN HARDER

If you're lucky to share a friend's table during high summer in the Catskills, you might be served tomatoes and corn as fine as anywhere on earth. Since 2015, Hannah Leighton and Christian Harder have been living close to the shape-shifting seasonal bounty of quiet Bovina. It's a blink-and-you'll-miss-it village with a population of 576 as of 2018—though that number has likely swelled since Bovina became a popular pandemic retreat for urban transplants seeking clean air and space to roam. Hannah is a researcher and community organizer focused on building a resilient local food system in her rural community and beyond. Her work focuses primarily on creating ecosystems that connect local farms to schools, hospitals, colleges, jails, and other institutions with mouths to feed. Chris is a photographer. I first saw his work while judging a competition in 2005, when he was twenty-four years

old. Sensing an affinity with his style and subjects, I hired him as my assistant, and for the next decade or so, we traversed the globe on assignment, from Mozambique to the high desert of Argentina. In the process, Chris was welcomed as an unofficial member of our family, becoming something of an older brother to my three kids. He is now a successful working artist whose practice aims to connect new generations to land and food. Hannah and Chris's two-story, mid-1800s farmhouse is the seat of their experiment in latter-day homesteading. It sits between Main Street and a small tributary of the Delaware River that swells each spring as snow and ice melt off the hills. They did most of the restoration work themselves. Outside, flower beds and strutting roosters form a rustic crown around the house. Neighbors gave them free rein over an unused plot nearby. They cultivate a more ambitious garden there, and each morning walk the quarter mile to harvest provisions. Chris studied marine biology and swam competitively growing up, which might explain the nautical economy of space and supplies in their ship-like kitchen. A principle of warm utility guides the curation and application of objects throughout the house. Small tables were gifted by Hannah's godmother. A collection of vinyl records inherited from Chris's father stack neatly in the living room. Delta blues crackled like summer rain from the turntable the day I visited. We ate lunch around a German beer-hall table outside: tomato sandwiches, green beans, salad, and corn and peppers grilled by Chris. With these two, I'm confident such impressive spreads are standard fare. Food is the very warp and weft of their intertwined life, which to me exemplifies the respectful adoption of these remote places as settings for new ways of living in a world that often alienates us from our food, and the earth from which it's born.

HAL PHILIPPS + GREG KENDALL

From Wadi Rum to Santorini to Fogo Island, my eyes and lens have long been drawn to the geology of places I have been very fortunate to visit. Sites that reveal the substance of the earth itself have a way of putting unthinkable spans of time in perspective, dwarfing the whole sweep of human history, let alone the fleeting trials and triumphs of daily life. With its sculptural boulders and cliffs of limestone, sandstone, and shale, the Hudson Valley is a geologist's playground, and on the slopes of Mount Merino, south of Hudson, sits a home that stirs that sense of earthly wonder in me. Its owners purchased the lot sight unseen in 2013, spending the first year patiently hammering into dense bedrock to prepare for construction and habitation. Into this cradle was poured five million pounds of locally produced concrete: the raw matter of a striking structure inspired by Brutalist architecture and the industrial history of Hudson, designed by New York's KOKO. As with Frederic Church's Olana (see pages 112–23),

which is situated on a neighboring slope to the south, the owners carefully captured panoramic views of the river, the Catskill Mountains, the Berkshires, and the lush gardens and meadows they planted on either side of the house. The interior rivals the exterior environment with a breathtaking collection of art, furniture, and objects. Stationed like an attentive butler by the door is a dazzling *Soundsuit* by Nick Cave. At the sculpture's back, a glassed-in interior courtyard is planted with ferns and grasses like a diorama of prehistoric America, accentuated by a mahogany sculpture by Ben Butler, set among the underbrush, resembling the vertebrae of a fossilized creature. Toward a curved corridor to the left, a series of black butterfly sculptures by Paul Villinski dots the undulating wall above the Steinway piano. These graceful insects are a recurring motif in the house, contributing to the sense that it is a vast concrete chrysalis: a space that, despite its imposing presence, is brimming with delicate life, existing in a state of continuous transition and constantly morphing as a result of the mercurial patterns of weather and light outside. Like the geologic formation into which it's built, the house is deeply planted in the earth, as if to bear witness to the passage of time.

ACKNOWLEDGMENTS

I dedicate this book to my father,
William Abranowicz.
He would have loved this place.

I am especially thankful to each of the subjects whose personal spaces were given over to me to photograph for this book. I'd also like to thank the people who kindly gave me opportunity as well as their time and consideration: Amy Astley; Dominique Browning; Sarah Boyd; Malcolm Buick, Dara Caponigro, Stephanie Diaz, and Hudson Moore of Frederic / Schumacher; Caroline Crumpacker of Opus 40; Alan Cumming; Susan and Tom Engel; Manuel Frei; Lucy Gilmour; Jennifer Greim, Amanda Malmstrom, Heather Paroubek, and Kate Menconeri at the Thomas Cole House; Amy Ilias and Jim Denney; Anne Johnson; Vicky Lowry; Janeen Martin and Amy Hausmann at Olana; Maura McEvoy; Frank Mentessena; Jeffrey Miller; Chris, Nepal, and Nino Mottalini; Heather Phelps-Lipton; Tobey Poser and John Adams; Michael Reynolds; Peter Ross: Michelle Saunders; Priscilla Woolworth and Anthony Slater-Ralph.

Zander Abranowicz, my son and collaborator, took random, disconnected thoughts and reactions that I cryptically passed to him and beautifully expressed what I wanted to articulate but could not. This is our third book together. His words get more beautiful each time and his vast knowledge of art and the visual process surprised me at every turn. Zander's willingness to work on another book with his old man is a blessing I cherish dearly. My wife, Andrea, spent many evenings with the work. Her thoughtful critiques could infuriate me, but she was usually right, and laughing through disagreements made stressful work better and the process fun. Taylor, Zander's wife, is to be thanked for her cheerful support and love during this time. Simon Abranowicz designed the typeface and looked at every iteration of the work with the eye, acuity, and thoughtfulness of a great teacher. Max, my daughter, was always there for her papa even when she was living in Palermo. Thanks to Anne Kennedy, Becky Lewis, Reina Nakagawa, Page Phillips, and Michael Van Horne of my agency, Art + Commerce, who helped to get this project off the ground and hold it there.

I am extremely grateful for the opportunity I was given by Mark Magowan, who approached me to do this work. Mark lent suggestions and provided brilliant guidance and optimism throughout. Being able to remain home, rather than traveling as is my norm, was a rare gift. Along with Beatrice Vincenzini and Francesco Venturi at Vendome, their enthusiasm and support are a dream. I love knowing that the work finds itself in the best hands. Losing loved images or words during editing is the hardest part of the process, but Jackie Decter glided through reviews like a brilliant surgeon, with minimal discomfort and an end result that felt so right. Celia Fuller, the book's designer, worked in a way that coalesced perfectly with my hope for the design. She knows all the rules and twists and breaks them as needed to make something new. The ever-affable Jim Spivey always handles the complexities of production flawlessly. Each of these people leads me to say I am proud to be part of the Vendome family.

And lastly, to my mother, Margaret, who passed away during the making of this work. Every time I look at the pink of the sun on these mountains around me, I think of her.

Country Life: Homes of the Catskill Mountains and Hudson Valley
First published in 2023 by The Vendome Press
Vendome is a registered trademark of The Vendome Press LLC

VENDOME PRESS US
P.O. Box 566
Palm Beach, FL 33480

VENDOME PRESS UK
Worlds End Studio
132–134 Lots Road
London, SW10 0RJ

www.vendomepress.com

Distributed in North America by Abrams Books
Distributed in the United Kingdom, and the rest of the world, by Thames & Hudson

ISBN 978-0-86565-431-0

PUBLISHERS: Beatrice Vincenzini, Mark Magowan, and Francesco Venturi
EDITOR: Jacqueline Decter
PRODUCTION DIRECTOR: Jim Spivey
DESIGNER: Celia Fuller

Library of Congress Cataloging-in-Publication Data
available upon request

Printed and bound in China by
1010 Printing International Ltd.

FIRST PRINTING